Three
I's

Andrew Z Carroll

The Three I's

Copyright Notice
The Three I's

For information on bulk orders or to have Andrew Carroll speak at your event, please contact below:

Andrew Carroll Presents
Email: Andrew@andrewcarrollpresents.com
Website: www.andrewcarrollpresents.com

ISBN: 9781093965384

The Three I's

DEDICATION

My three little bears; Daddy loves you. Always.

I love you, Mom.

Oma and Papa I love you and work to make you proud daily.

Alphabet Soup, I am grateful for all of you:
TWC, JEC, SPC, TAC, ESC, SWC, HEC, JTP, CSL, CK, JB,
TW, JW, PW, CR, TR, PB, JB, DE, SP, WL, PA, BW, BM,
MF

The Three I's

CONTENTS

The Three I's

ACKNOWLEDGMENTS

Thank you Brandon Allen. Without you this would have never become a reality. Your investment in me put me on a path of growth and self-actualization.

FORWARD

If you looked at me as simply the mistakes I have made you might wonder how I was able to accomplish anything in my life. I was expelled from high school and sent to rehab. I was laughed out of an Air Force recruiting office. I was arrested and placed on felony probation for selling a small amount of marijuana and I've been arrested for DUI. I have been divorced twice and filed bankruptcy. I've had a motorcycle repossessed and I've spent a summer at in-patient rehab/therapy at the VA. I cheated on my wife numerous times and stayed in a toxic relationship "for the kids".

If this was all you knew about me you would probably say I was total human garbage.

Trust me, I totally understand. I believed I was an awful man with no prospects or motivation. A deadbeat. A burnout. Maybe even a criminal. I felt useless. I knew in my heart that I added zero value. That everyone I knew would be better off without me. I defined myself by my failures. I was ashamed of myself all day, every day. Anxiety, depression and suicidal ideations were my normal. When I crawled out of that haze long enough to take a few deep breaths of positivity it wouldn't be long before my inner voice would say, "You've been doing well long enough. We better mess this up before you get to comfortable."

Next thing you know I'd be doing something awful, pushing the boundaries of acceptable behavior. All for the momentary rush of feeling like I was alive. Generally, this behavior would involve some external validation from people I had no business talking to as a married man, drinking myself into a stupor for months at a time or abusing medication. Regardless of where or what I was doing I would be self-sabotaging because I didn't feel like I deserved to be successful.

However, if we had spoken back then it is likely I would have said all the right things. I would have seemed confident and friendly. I worked very hard on the appearance of having it together. I smiled a lot and was funny enough. People never tend to dig when you're funny. For most of my life humor was a defense mechanism to keep people from asking me tough questions. I didn't like to have feelings and I certainly didn't like talking about them.

I lived a life of numbness and insecurity for decades. From the first time I was made to feel small at five years old by a little boy who had learned racism at home until I was crushed to my rock bottom at 31 years old, I lived in darkness. Through all of this, my only reprieve was humor. I didn't recognize this for what it was when I was younger but I have a better understanding of that now.

I get so many comments from people who used to know me that go along the lines of, "Wow, I had no idea you were struggling like that. You were always kind and funny. The best smile I've ever seen!" Well, thanks for saying that, I do have a great smile. It served me well as a shield to keep people out of my business. I've missed out on so much of life because I didn't live for myself. I didn't do what was best for Andrew because I was worried about what other people would think of me. I didn't want to offend anyone or step on toes. The beauty of everything I have been through? I refuse to live that life anymore. I do what is good for me and I am growing in all kinds of amazing directions because of this!

As you read this book it is my hope that you will be able to identify areas in your life that you want to improve and then implement an intelligent, intentional and immediate change in your life. I want the best for you but that is not enough. You have to want the best for you! I promise you that with hard work and consistency you, too, can elevate your life beyond your wildest imagination.

Chapter 1 - My Mom

She placed two hands on the cold concrete and pulled herself up on to the barrier of the freeway overpass. Heart pounding she thought of all the things in her life that she loved, all the things she was about to leave behind and the pain that she would forever escape. As she closed her eyes and readied herself to jump the baby in her stomach moved. This gentle reminder to his mother that she was not alone.

He spent the majority of his time abusing her. On numerous occasions, he tried to murder her. The physical, mental and emotional abuse give a glimpse into why she chose to climb onto that barrier. As the baby moved inside her stomach she chose life. She climbed down off of that barrier, found a payphone and called her parents. Together they coordinated a plan for her to escape in the night. She would no longer be under the control of a madman.

I was born in northern Idaho, blue with an umbilical cord wrapped around my neck. The attending physician left the room because I was not a white child. Fortunately, another doctor stepped in and saved me. Before I was even born my mom set the example or what it means to love someone. She was starting completely over. Now a single mother with a mixed-race baby in northern Idaho in 1985.

Much before I can remember we relocated to the Tacoma area. My mom attended Pacific Lutheran University. Some of my first memories include her reading textbooks to me. I was blessed for all of these moments. I was blessed to be alive and so was she. Over the next several years my mom would complete a bachelor's and master's degree while raising me with help from my grandparents. The sacrifices and obstacles that my mother overcame were significant. Everything I do is dedicated to my mom. She has loved me unconditionally since before I took my first breath. In the aftermath of every mistake I have ever made she has been there for me. My mom has done the best she could for me since the moment I took my first raggedy breath as a blue infant in a hospital room where I wasn't wanted by anyone but her.

I am so blessed to have her Warrior Spirit within me. It is because of her example that I will be successful in all that I do. My mom has touched the lives of countless people across the United States and the world. She has always been an educator in the truest sense of the word. She loves every student that comes into her classroom or attends her school. She believes that every child deserves an equal opportunity to learn and she specializes in helping kids with learning difficulties get the most out of their education. In her classroom, no child is ever left behind. I am constantly reminded that a smart man is only as smart as the woman he keeps company with. Women like my mom have blazed a trail for my daughters.

Without the love my mom gave me unconditionally throughout my life it is very likely I wouldn't have made it through my self-imposed hardships. She is incredibly important and I want to publicly thank her for all she has done and continues to do for me.

Get Grateful!

Who is important in your life? Who are you grateful for? Who had an immense impact, in a positive way, for you? Get out a notebook and a pen and write down the names of people for whom you are grateful. Are you struggling? That is absolutely okay. Even if you can only think of one person write down their name. Now, write WHY you are grateful for this person or these people. It doesn't have to be a letter but it is absolutely okay if it is! Remember, we are never truly alone on this journey.

Chapter 2 - Denton

Most of my life has been spent trying to prove to other people that I'm not a statistic or the stereotype they expect me to be. It is kind of ironic that all the effort I was putting in to not be a stereotype actually ended up causing me to be a statistic. I was a troubled kid but not because I had a bad home life. My mom loves me unconditionally regardless of my behavior.

She remarried when I was 13 years old we moved about 36 miles away from my friends and the school where she worked and I attended. The best things in my life at the time were my relationships with a few select people who saw value within me that I didn't recognize. The Barber's opened their home so that I could stay with them on weekends and during the school week if I wanted to. The Reid's and Wickens' are, to this day, the kindest people you will ever meet. I was blessed to have a few amazing teachers that had a huge impact on my early education. A very small circle of about four people were who I called my best friends. I will always be grateful for everything they blessed me with.

My life at home wasn't bad by any means but the man my mom chose to marry did not care much for me. In fact, he had asked my mom to tell me not to hug him. This might seem pretty simple but that set the tone for how I knew he felt about me for the rest of my time living in that house. However, it was great to have a ranch where I could ride a dirt bike and shoot guns all day. Working with livestock, fencing and even the few times I got to help with harvest ended up being some of my favorite activities. I learned the value of hard work through these experiences. As a kid, I put more effort into getting out of work and screwing around.

At about 14 years old I started drinking and smoking marijuana. I had a few friends that would join me in a smoke and we were happy in our circle. We socialized more often outside of our circle when we could get some alcohol. In a town of 300 people you can't do much without everybody finding out. So, in general, all the plans that I thought were so sneaky usually ended up as a Monday morning highlight for my mom. Eventually, I was allowed to use my mom's car more or less anytime I wanted unless I was grounded. Like I mentioned I would spend as much time as I could in Denton because my girlfriend and my best friends lived there.

I want to make something very clear; growing up in Denton provided its own unique set of challenges however, I wouldn't trade it for anything in the world. I try not to dwell on my past but I often find myself wondering how much more trouble I would have gotten into had I lived in a city or anywhere else for that matter. Would I have still felt so different and alone? Would I have had more access to art and culture? Would I have gotten an education equal to that of a classroom with a 7 to 1 student teacher ratio? I'll never be able to answer these questions. What I do know is that I'm grateful for every triumph and failure that I experienced growing up in my little town. Denton, Montana will forever be my home and the people there will always have a special place in my heart.

At the end of the day my group of friends and I never really caused any real trouble.

Another fortunate thing about growing up in a small town is that it really is a community. So when my friends and I did get in trouble it was because we did something stupid, got caught and that group of adults would talk to our parents so in general the cops never got called... except for that one time.

During the basketball season in my small town, you could be sure that almost every house was empty. A few of my friends and I decided that it would be fun to see how much beer we could get a hold of. As no one locked their doors we ended up with something like 10 cases of beer and a bottle of Crown Royal. What do you do with this much free beer you ask? Well, you wait for the basketball game to be over and you hand out beers to every other teenager in town until you have a pretty decent party going on.

This was all fun and games over the weekend and then Monday rolled around. This time people did call the cops. We ended up on juvenile probation doing community service for the summer. Back then we viewed it as a pretty harmless prank. The consequences taught me some pretty good lessons. The thing about juvenile probation is you meet other kids who are way more experienced at doing illegal stuff than you are. I learned a lot about how to get away with certain things, how people got caught for certain things and that I should be grateful that I was loved at home.

Trouble Maker

Take a moment to reflect on times in your youth that you caused some trouble. Now using our trusted notebook I want you to write down a few of these moments. Did you get caught? What did you learn? Have you evaluated how that has shaped you up to this point in your life? I want you to spend some time considering what you would tell yourself before and after the moments you have written down. Once you know what you would like to say I want you to write it in the notebook. Remember, we are working on growth so be compassionate and kind to younger you!

Chapter 3 - Arlington, Whitehall, Indio

The first time I was caught smoking pot at school I was in Arlington, Washington living with my Uncle. He had one rule: you can't smoke pot if you are going to live here. It was a great rule because he was gone, busting his ass for his family 90% of the time. When he was home I wouldn't smoke pot. The rest of the time? Game on.

The drive back to his house after we talked to the principal together was one of the worst of my life. I always looked up to my Uncle and he had always been amazing to me. The worst part of the whole experience was letting him down. When we got back to the house I got my pipe and the rest of the pot I had. We went into the bathroom and he watched me flush my stash. Then we went into the garage and smashed my pipe with a hammer. I was on a plane back to Montana the next day.

The second time I got caught smoking pot at school would be the end of my high school "career" if you could call it that. It was January 2003 and I had just turned 17. My friend wasn't allowed to leave campus at lunch because he had gotten a speeding ticket a week or two prior over the lunch period. We walked out behind the bus barn, smoked a bowl and went about our business. As luck would have it the Principal was in the Crow's Nest overlooking the football field with a video camera. He caught us red-handed, dead to rights.

This time I was called into the office alone. I had the pot stashed in my jacket and as he sat that for what felt like an eternity trying to find the hidden zipper to get the pot out all I could think to myself was was a word not suitable for print. I was expelled from High School that day. Within a couple of weeks I was in inpatient rehab at Rimrock Foundation in Billings, MT. All I knew about my future was that I would be moving to California to live with my grandparents as soon as I was finished with the 30-day program.

Rehab was my first real experience of learning how to dig into my thoughts and feelings. I had been numbing myself since I was 13. This program was actually a great experience because for the first time I felt like I had a shot to make something of myself. I didn't know what I would make but I knew a fresh start in California with my grandparents would change everything.

I had been living in California for a few months working two jobs and enjoying the feeling of having more money than I knew what to do with. However, I knew that I didn't want to work for a certain giant box store or a golf course for the rest of my life. I needed to make something of myself. One morning I woke up and decided I was going to join the Air Force. I was still on juvenile probation for smoking pot at school but I figured they used to let people pick prison or the military so I had a shot!

I went to talk to the local recruiter and told him all about myself. He looked at me and said, "There is no way we can get you in." I didn't have a GED, I was on juvenile probation and I was 17. I begged. I pleaded. I asked a million more questions. I told him how serious I was about joining. Finally, he gave me an inch and that was all I needed. He scheduled me for the

ASVAB and I got a 92 overall. I sat for my GED and crushed that, too. I reached out to my juvenile probation officer and worked out a deal that they would let me off probation if the Air Force accepted me. I was going to make something of myself, finally. In May of 2004 I was shipped off to Lackland Air Force Base, Texas to begin my military career.

Substance Use

Have you ever used drugs, alcohol or anything else to help you cope? I understand the urge to do so. So many of us in America have dealt with or are dealing with unhealthy relationships with substances or activities. As a kid I always just wanted adults to be honest with me about drugs, alcohol and sex. However, any time I would bring it up all I was ever told regarding alcohol and drugs was they were bad and sex was for marriage. This didn't help me understand or develop a responsible attitude towards any of these things.

Get out your notebook, it's time for you to write! I want you to consider what you would want to tell yourself about drugs, alcohol and sex when you were younger. Write it in your notebook as a letter to your past self. Be real. Be vulnerable. Be honest.

Chapter 4 - The Air Force

I knew the Air Force would change my life but I never really understood how much until it was over. Basic training and Tech School last from May to December of 2004. I arrived at Offutt Air Force Base as a married 18-year-old Airman. Offutt was a learning experience that shaped the rest of my career and my personal life in a big way. I got involved with some individuals and an organization that resulted in investigations, confidential informants and the death of a mentor and friend. As a result, I felt guilty for years. Through counseling and therapy I eventually released that guilt. I did the right thing; exhibited the Air Force Core Value of Integrity First. I was ostracized from my unit for my decision to speak up. Fortunately, I left for a new assignment in October 2006. Unfortunately, it was as a 20-year-old dad going through a divorce.

RAF Mildenhall was an amazing experience for me both personally and professionally. I left the past behind in Nebraska and really enjoyed my time in England. For the next 2 years I worked, played rugby and partied. I was in a relationship with my High School sweetheart and we were already on a rocky foundation from the start. We had a lot of fun but we also had a lot of problems. It's hard to be in love with the "idea" of someone. Expectations are a killer.

In November of 2008 we moved to Germany. If I could go anywhere in the world again it would be here. I absolutely loved it there. My assignment had me in a small Post Office at Kapaun Air Base. I worked with some absolutely stellar people during this time. We were a family. Sometimes we didn't get along but everyone knew their role, took care of business and we looked out for each other. In the small village of Schallodenbach my wife and I were adopted by our German neighbors Gatz and Bettina. Their family became our family.

When our daughter Alora was born Gatz and Bettina became Oma and Papa.

My wife and I had even more problems while we lived in Germany, though. Our relationship was nothing but ups and downs. An intensity that is hard to describe defined the toxicity that had been brewing between us since we had started dating again in 2006. But we kept at it. Thinking that we were living a fairy tale. A love story for the ages. We weren't.

In 2011 we were still in Germany but the end of my enlistment was coming up and I had some choices to make. I knew from the day I put on my uniform that if I hit ten years of service I would stay in. I didn't want to be in the Postal career field for the rest of my life and I began applying for cross-training opportunities. I wasn't picked up for any of the jobs I requested so I started looking at which bases I could go to and perform my primary duty as a telephone systems technician. I was denied all ten bases I requested.

I took this as some sort of sign and started researching colleges. I talked to my wife about where we could go and she was adamant about moving home to Montana. I wanted to go to Missoula but she insisted on Bozeman. I applied to Montana State University and was actually accepted. I was incredibly surprised by this but ecstatic nonetheless. I submitted a request to separate from the Air Force in August of 2011 so I could start the school year in the fall. My commander granted this request and in July we were back in Montana.

Leaving the safety and security of Active Duty Military service was a legitimate shock. I had my GI BIll and my wife had a job, too. Without the structure I had become so accustomed to I once again fell back into my old habits. When I was active duty I drank often and hard. Now that I was a civilian I could return to my drug of choice, marijuana. Boy did I ever take advantage of that. I got my medical card and was able to purchase marijuana legally. Without the structure I was accustomed to I really started to unravel.

Freedom

When was the last time you found yourself with an unusual or unfamiliar sense of freedom? Did you get out of the military? Perhaps you just got out of a long term relationship. Maybe you just finished serving time on probation, jail or prison. I want you to write down a few times when you have felt this way. We will use it at the end of the next chapter for another exercise!

Chapter 5 - College and Probation

My first major in college was Health and Human Performance. I thought it would be a lot of fun learning how to train people and maximize my time in the gym. What I discovered was that I actually hated almost all of the foundational coursework. By the end of my first semester I had switched to Marketing. I thought I would be learning to create advertising campaigns. I couldn't have been more wrong! The best part of Marketing was that it forced me into an Economics course. I changed my major again and for the next 3 years I studied Economics.

I thought this would be a degree that would open all kinds of doors. It has, but none of them are in the field of Economics. It was the hardest academic achievement I've accomplished to date. Learning calculus took me so much time outside of class. Thank God for Brandon helping me figure things out.

I got a job with the IT department on campus and worked part-time while I was a full-time student year round. I also spent a ton of time working running, swimming, and lifting. Even though I was getting high almost every day I had this idea in my heart that I would end up back in the Air Force as an officer or I would get into S.E.R.E. or Combat Control. I was putting in the physical effort to achieve these goals and got myself in the best shape of my life over the next year.

From fall 2011 to summer 2012 I was preparing myself to apply for an Air Force Reserve enlistment as Combat Control. The physical requirements to even be considered are rigorous and challenge even the fittest individuals. I had everything under control. I was beating the minimum score for each portion of the test by a solid margin. I was in the best shape of my life at that time. I reached out to the MSU Rugby Club and went to my first practice with the team. The practice was going extremely well and I was feeling strong. I caught a pass and there was an opening between a couple of defenders and I slipped through. I was being attacked from 3 o'clock and I made a hard cut instead of powering forward. I slipped that defender and on my second step into my sprint away I felt what I thought was a "flat tire" from a defender stepping on my heel and pulling off my shoe. More concerning, though, was the simultaneous feeling of a massive cable snapping inside of my body. Imagine that vibrating cable snapping sound in the movies. It felt exactly like that. I tried to keep running but had lost all power production from my left leg. I tried walking it off but after about 10 meters I had to sit down. I told some of the boys what had happened and that I think I needed to go to the hospital. I tried to drive but I had a WRX with a manual transmission and a stiff clutch. I couldn't push the clutch at all.

My best friend Jake picked me up and took me to the emergency room. As soon as I talked to the doc and he examined my leg he confirmed my biggest fear, "You've got a ruptured Achilles tendon." I had been pretty well drugged but I was devastated. The physical punishment I had put myself through. The countless miles pounding the pavement, lifting heavy weights, swimming daily. Even my diet was solid and pretty dialed in. For over a year I had been hammering my body into a machine. I ate, slept and breathed training for an opportunity to become an Air Force Combat Controller.

Now, in the blink of an eye, it was taken away. I would be couch bound and non-weight bearing for at least 3 months. My plan was ruined. My effort felt wasted. The mental benefit of working out would be lost. I was referred to an Orthopedic Surgeon and surgery was scheduled.

During this time I was also a full-time student and working for the IT department at Montana State. I continued to work and attend class as best I could. One blessing I recognized right away was that I was in great shape and crutching around from class to class all over campus wasn't nearly as difficult as it would have been otherwise. The injury and recovery would have been significantly more difficult to manage if I hadn't been fit and healthy.

In June or July I got a phone call out of the blue from a detective asking me to come to the station for an interview. My heart jumped into my throat but I agreed to go. The detective came called my name and I followed him into an interrogation room. We sat down and he began to do his job. It soon became obvious that they had been watching me for a while and knew I was selling small amounts of marijuana to close friends. This was something I never thought law enforcement would care about. I was, even in the most exaggerated terms, "small potatoes". The detective, a part of the Missouri River Drug Task Force, made me an offer; find three other people selling drugs and they would give me my file and nothing would happen to me. I already knew I wouldn't do that but I asked for some time to consider things. What I really wanted time for was finding a lawyer. I figured based on what the detective had said to me that worst case scenario I'd get hit with a misdemeanor after my lawyer did his/her job.

First of all, I want to say that I broke the law. I decided to take my chances with the legal system. I was not about to turn snitch on people selling marijuana. I do not regret taking my punishment because I kept my integrity intact. When I finally got with my attorney he said it would be no problem to get a deal and have all the charges reduced. He also told me to stop talking to the police, so I did.

About a month passed by and I got another call out of the blue. It was the detective, "Andrew, you've had some time to think and I wanted to see what you'd come up with for us." It was not a question, it was a statement. I replied that I had retained an attorney and had been advised not to speak with him anymore. This was right around August of 2012. September, October, and November passed without word from my lawyer or the detective. I figured it was being handled and was able to keep my focus on school, work and my family during this time.

Right before Christmas I got an odd call from my wife, "Hey, I just wanted to let you know the cops were just here looking for you." I asked if they had left any contact info or anything and she gave me a phone number. I suppose I should have called my lawyer but I called the number the police had left with my wife. I offered to come down to the station but they told me to stay at work and they would come to see me. I understood and would be in the office when they arrived.

The crackle of a police radio was the sound that welcomed me into a moment I will never forget. As I stood up, trying to mentally prepare myself for what I guessed would be my arrest I was taken aback by the number of officers that appeared in the hallway. I was one guy, a risk to no one and there were at least four police officers here to get me. By now I had seen the evidence against me. I was being arrested for selling one-eighth of an ounce of marijuana (three paper clips weigh roughly the same amount) to a fellow student named Nathan. I am sure he was offered the same deal I had been offered. The major difference being that I hadn't taken the deal. The point? Four to six police officers show up to arrest me, an alleged non-violent drug offender, for selling a small amount of marijuana to an informant. I would have just turned myself in if they had asked.

As I stood up I looked the officer in the eye and approached with my hand outstretched and introduced myself, "Hi, I'm Andrew Carroll. I believe you're looking for me, sir." As I was asked to turn around and place my hands behind my back I started to wonder what came next. Would I be stuck in a jail cell all weekend? I hoped not. I don't belong in jail. I've been twice, only briefly, and I'm not a fan. I was processed at the station and was able to make a phone call and bail out of the jail in about an hour.

I don't remember exactly what happened next but at some point soon after that I was made to register for pre-trial diversion. This is an interesting little program. Consider the following; you are innocent until proven guilty. I had not been to trial, I had only been charged with

Criminal Distribution of a Dangerous Drug - Marijuana. I had not been convicted. Pre-trial diversion required that I call into a number every day to see if my "color" had been announced. If my color had been announced I was then to report by 10 am to my supervision and submit to a urinalysis and breathalyzer test. I would, at a minimum, do this once per week. I got to play this game for six months before I even went to trial. Six months, while I was supposed to be presumed innocent, I was living on more rigid conditions than I would be while on probation. When I finally went to trial I was amazed at how impersonal it all was. All anyone cared about was the fact that I had broken the law. The deal my lawyer got me was one day in jail, for which I was credited my time, and 2 years of deferred felony probation. I was just happy not to go back to jail. I wasn't going to be a felon as long as I successfully completed the terms of my probation; No guns, drugs, alcohol or legal entanglements for two years.

The most important thing I learned being on probation was how it feels to have your life completely controlled by one individual. For the first 12 months of my probation, I was at the beck and call of a man who viewed the world as black and white with absolutely no sense of humor. I never felt like a person under his supervision. He made me feel worthless. It felt like all of the hard work and effort that I put into my life raising my family, working, running a business and as a full-time student meant nothing. To my probation officer, I was a scumbag who had sold some marijuana and deserved the full weight of the legal system to be brought down upon me.

This led to a constant feeling of anxiety, depression and suicidal ideation. I lived each day feeling like I was worthless. The weekend before college graduation my wife and I got into a huge fight. As a poor response to our argument I decided to take some pills and drink. I sank deeper and deeper into my feelings. I reached out to a friend as I was struggling with thoughts of hurting myself. Thank God for Andrew. From across the country he reached out to the police department in Bozeman, Montana and asked for a welfare check. When the police arrived I spoke with them and admitted to drinking and told them what was going on. They escorted me to the hospital and I was evaluated to make sure that I was in a mental state to be released back to my home. The psychologist cleared me to go and I was not taken to jail that night. In the morning a probation officer that was filling in for my guy came and checked on me. She had a heart and was kind enough to tell me that I would still be able to go to graduation and I wouldn't be going to jail. My regular probation officer was out of town.

Graduating from college is the only time I have ever finished anything academically in the traditional sense. I did just fine and Technical School when I joined the Air Force but actually walking across the stage and accepting a diploma is something I had never done before. College was incredibly hard for me. I struggled on a daily basis to understand my homework and the concepts that were being taught in class. By the time I got to college in 2011 I had not been in a formal classroom setting for almost 10 years. It was a very difficult transition for me.

The point; graduating from college was a huge deal to me and by the grace of God I was able to walk across that stage and accept my diploma even after I had broken the conditions of my probation. When this incident happened I was on track to do halftime. Halftime is when you are successful in your probation and you only have to serve half of your original sentence. When I graduated I was only two months being allowed my halftime opportunity.

My poor choices ended up giving me another 14 months of probation time. When I went for my second to last appointment with my probation officer he made it very clear to me that if he had been working when I had been taken to the hospital I would have spent the weekend in jail and wouldn't have been able to graduate. He made me feel small for the last time in that office.

I had already applied and been accepted to inpatient treatment at the Sheridan VA for the summer of 2014 as a result of the incident that broke my probation. I was to be released to the custody of the Sheridan VA and would be under their supervision until such time that I moved to Billings Montana. The staff at the VA in Sheridan Wyoming were fantastic to me. Near the end of my six to eight weeks there I was elected as president of the Resident Veterans Council. I became the liaison between the veterans in residence and the facility staff and leadership.

This was a point of pride for me as it was one of the first times in my entire life my character, integrity, and personality had earned me a position as a leader among my peers. During my time in inpatient treatment people got to know me intimately. I became known as a positive and compassionate member of the team. A few weeks later I bid farewell to my friends and the faculty that had helped me so much along my way.

After the Sheridan VA I moved to Billings, Montana with my wife and our two kids. My probation was transferred there and my new probation officer was a human with a heart. My new probation officer had such a huge impact on my renewed success. After having been under the thumb of a man who treated me like less than a number I couldn't have been more excited to be under the supervision of someone who actually saw me as a person. I was actively working to further grow and develop my life and career and take care of my family. The simple fact that I was being treated like a human made me feel that I needed to respect myself and the terms of my probation.

After another year of I successfully completed the terms of my probation. I was released and all rights were restored. I am not a felon. I truly believe a large part of that is because of the attitude and approach my final probation officer had toward his job and his true role in the process.

I was also blessed to be surrounded by a mom and family that loved and supported me even when I was being a idiot. If it weren't for the love they showed me in spite of all of my poor choices, I don't think I would have come out the other side of this experience with such little dirt to brush off my knees as I picked myself up to once again try and achieve my best life.

Self-Control

Time to get out your notebook! I want you to look at the times when you felt "unusual freedom". Now, I want you to consider how you handled those situations. Did you cut loose and go nuts or were you responsible and productive with your new freedom?

As I've shared with you here I allowed my lack of personal accountability to have a massive, negative impact on my life and my family. Were you better prepared to handle things than I was? Write down how you handled these situations and how you felt about the results. Identify if they were positive and healthy responses. If they weren't I want you to identify how you would do things differently if faced with a similar situation today.

Chapter 6 - Marriage

My relationship with my ex-wife was incredibly toxic. We met when we were 14 years old and became each others safe place. We were inseparable for a little over two years. We parted ways when I moved to Arlington, Washington. We stayed in touch a bit but she started dating someone else and we drifted apart. When we came back together at 21 years old we thought we were living a love story. Obviously neither one of us was the same person the other had fallen in love with at 14. Looking back on this now I can clearly see that we were setting each other up for failure.

.At the time it was "romantic" and "all we had ever wanted". So we stayed together for ten years and two babies. Almost from the very start we were toxic. I wasn't honest and she couldn't forgive me. This set the stage for some pretty heated arguments, awful communication and a complete lack of trust from both of us. Why did we stay together for so long? Neither one of us had had good examples of a relationship growing up. We also didn't love ourselves as individuals and sought validation from each other.

When things were good our relationship seemed pretty solid. But that only lasted for a brief period of time. We also had a trauma bond from our childhood as the result of something she had been through and never talked about with anyone but me. We were together with the best intentions but our behavior and emotions caused us to belittle and destroy one another. One thing I do have to say is that we made a seriously awesome parenting team 99% of the time. We have raised the best kids you'll ever meet and for that, I am grateful beyond measure.

Over the course of my relationship with her I was belittled and pushed away. As a result, I sought the attention of women outside of my marriage. This behavior was inexcusable and was the final straw that truly broke my family apart. After I was honest with her about what I had done we spent years trying to make it work, tearing each other's throats out and repeating the whole cycle over and over and over again. No matter what we tried to do we couldn't break the cycle.

One morning I walked into our kitchen and placed my ring on the counter. I told her I couldn't do it anymore and went to work. I wouldn't learn until later that was the gesture that hurt her more than anything I had ever done before. I had finally broken her.

Our divorce was finalized one day before our seven year wedding anniversary. We showed up separately and signed our papers. No tears were shed and I had moved out of the house already. We kept talking to each other and slowly but surely I moved back into the house. We were in some hellacious dimension of a relationship without it being a relationship. She would tell me we were both single nearly every day and at night we would sleep together.

After a couple of months of this, we sold our house. I moved into an apartment and she moved in with a cousin. I took the girls every other week and weekend. Since we lived in the same area this was relatively easy to do. After a few weeks she started spending the night and eventually we were basically all living together in my apartment. Right back to being in a non-relationship relationship.

For the past year she had talked about leaving everything behind and moving to Phoenix. I had originally dismissed this as a pipe dream but then she started applying for jobs there. I was working for the Department of Veterans Affairs at the time and so I began to scour the federal government job boards for work in Arizona. I was offered a job in Williams, Arizona and was given two weeks to show up. When I told her the great news she said, "I'm not moving down there for a little while." I asked numerous times, "You are for sure moving there, right? I don't want to take this job and have you guys stay here in Montana." She continued to assure me that she would be taking the kids and moving to Arizona.

I sold everything I owned that didn't fit in my WRX and made the move to Arizona in January of 2017. I wouldn't see my daughters again until July 2nd, 2017. I had to pay for the move to their move to Arizona or it wouldn't have happened. We fell right back in where we had left off; being in a non-relationship relationship. No trust, constant bickering, a flash of something good and then right back to destroying each other. It was familiar...comfortable.

I was earning very little money working for the Forest Service in Arizona but the amazing people like Ariel and Ivan enriched my life beyond measure. With their help, I began to love myself. I began to see that I had value. I began to grow. I forgave myself for my past and accepted that it is a huge part of who I am but it does not define me. In Ariel and Ivan I had people who valued me for who I am. Even though my ex-wife and I were still together in our awful way I was beginning to see that I could be happy. We deserved the best even in our darkness.

If she hadn't taken six months to move to Arizona I may not have begun to understand that the way we treated each other wasn't okay. By October 2017 it would be time to move again for a better job. I would invite her to come, bring our girls and start over in Utah.

Toxic

Notebook time. I want you to think back on two relationships. The first relationship you need to recall is the one that hurt you. The toxic relationship that was allowed to tear you down and take from you. Next, I want you to think about the relationship that enriched you (I hope you are still in this relationship!).

Now that you have those called up into memory I want you to write down what it was about toxic relationship that caused you to lose yourself. What behavior did you exhibit that allowed the toxicity to continue? Finally, I want you to write down the behavior and actions that enrich and fulfill you in the relationship that enriched you.

Have you got it? Excellent. Now you have a tangible reference for what you will and won't accept in a relationship!

Chapter 7 - Utah

Changes in my personal and professional life brought me to Utah in 2017. My kids and my ex-wife made the move with me. They were in a U-haul and I was in the motorhome that I planned on living in. This thing was an ancient behemoth, absolutely awful, but it was paid off and I knew I'd be able to save money on rent with this strategy.

The morning after we arrived in Utah my ex-wife put the kids in the U-haul, told me she was moving back to Montana and left me crying in the parking lot of Walmart. A few days later she told me she was sleeping with someone else. Blinded as I was by our toxic relationship I figured we could work through it. After all, I had cheated on her countless times.

I spent a day or two thinking on all of this when I was struck by a thought; what if this is really it? All this pain and heartache and misery could be over, finally. The key to actually ending it all was getting my ex-wife to actually break me. I have this hard-headed tendency to believe I can salvage any relationship. I struggle to let go or give up on people. So, I called her up and asked her for one final favor. "I know this is going to sound weird but I'll never get past our relationship if you don't truly break me. I need you to tell me everything about sleeping with this other guy. Everything. Don't leave anything out." After a bit more asking she finally agreed and began telling me about their adventure. Surely they both had more fun than I did reliving the experience with her. However, when it was all over I thanked her for telling me the truth. With calm tears in my eyes, I said goodbye and hung up the phone.

As I sat in my motorhome staring at nothing I began to think. For the first time in my life, I felt completely alone. It was a bizarre feeling. I examined my heartache and began to think about what I could possibly do to alleviate the all-encompassing physical pain I was experiencing. I thought about the pistol in the bedroom. How I could go finish my work on this planet. I thought about this for longer than I would like to admit. Then, out of nowhere, the question "What if you chose to live, Andrew?" popped into my head. This was a stunning proposition to me at the time. Where did this challenge come from? I didn't want to live. I wanted to die. I felt pain, physical pain, because I was so emotionally, mentally and spiritually destroyed.

I rose from my couch, grabbed a cigarette and went outside into the cold dark night. The flame from the lighter dazzled my vision. I thought about all the crap I had been through. All of the self-sabotage. All of the poor choices. My cycle of destroying what I valued out of some innate fear I had of losing control. With each drag on that cigarette, I steeled my resolve. "I'm better than I've been. What's the point of this life if I never choose to live it? I'm done with all that. I am going to live. I'm going to use what I've done to help others. I'm going to make the absolute most out of where I am and what I'm doing."

I decided right then and there that I loved myself. That I did have value. That I wasn't defined by the things I had done or where I had failed but by what I had achieved. I have risen from the ashes of my self-immolation time and time again.

Rock Bottom

Time to really dig deep. Have you felt rock bottom before? What was that like for you? How did you react? It is time to write down one of the most difficult moments in your life. As you do this I want you to consider the self-sabotaging behaviors you perpetuated to get there. We are responsible for how we react, no one else. Take responsibility for this. Own it. Because you are BETTER THAN YOU HAVE BEEN!

Chapter 8 - The Beginning

The next morning I laced up my Chucks, got out my lifting program and hit the gym. I was humbled. It had been at least 6 months since I had really lifted weights. I had set that passion aside over the summer to learn to skateboard with my son. It showed. I was still right at 230 pounds but I was soft, squishy, gelatinous, pudgy...fluffy. I took a selfie in the mirror at the RV park I was living in so I would never forget that moment. I made a commitment right there on the spot to fix my body. It was all within my control. My interior health would be reflected in my appearance. I got serious about my diet as well. Heavy weight training, conditioning work, and a pretty solid nutrition plan. I was on a mission to change my composition and not necessarily lose weight. From October 2017 to July 2018 my change was significant. The most beautiful part of all of this? My mental, spiritual and emotional health were all improving as well.

I got in touch with the Pastoral team at Christian Life Center in Layton, Utah. I made an appointment with the Care team and began building my relationship with this local church. I volunteered to work at the Winter Jam concert in Salt Lake City. For a short time, I worked with Family Promise Ministry. Then I was recruited to join the Stephen Ministry. Stephen Ministry and the people I went through training with are one of the biggest factors of my success in overcoming the darkest darkness of my entire life. I was, for the first time in my life, mindfully working on my spiritual health and my relationship with God.

Meditation and journaling became staple activities for my daily life. I focused on the affirmations of self-love and compassion. I focused on radiating my love outward to those around me. I focused on being a conduit of compassion, kindness, and humility to those I came into contact with. I worked daily to love my feelings and emotions. I strived to understand "why" I would feel a certain way, a type of soulful root cause analysis of my own psyche. As I grew to love and understand myself more the universe continued to open up to me. A simple seeker was blessed to become a traveler among the stars of his own consciousness. This insight into myself isn't something that happened overnight and it is certainly a skill that evaporates like water on a Phoenix sidewalk. Intentionally practicing meditation and journaling will build up your mind and soul much like lifting weights builds your muscles.

Chapter 9 - The Work

If it isn't evident by now I used to excel at getting in my own way. The night that I chose to live I came to the realization that I needed to stop unhealthy habits and self-sabotaging cyclical behavior. What does this mean? First and foremost it meant that I needed to replace unhealthy habits with healthy habits. I did an in-depth break down of what I was doing with my life. At the time I was not working out consistently, eating a pretty poor diet, staying out too late and spending time with people that didn't build me up. By analyzing my situation in this way I was able to come up with a plan. First, I began with the understanding that progress takes time but an intelligent approach and intentional actions applied immediately would maximize the return on my investment in myself.

For roughly 10 years I had been lifting weights and reading about fitness in some way shape or form. I also had pretty great success following a strict cyclical ketogenic diet to lose body fat. I made the commitment to planning out my workouts to include heavy compound lifts and a cleaner diet so that I would be physically healthy.

The next step was to begin journaling positive affirmations so that I could change my mindset about myself. A lot of people do not know this next part; I absolutely hated myself. I had become so focused on all the negative things in my life I couldn't begin to appreciate the effort and success that I had managed to cobble together even in my past. Through journaling positive affirmations I had taken up the mindful practice of self-love. Consistency and time created a change in my mindset. Now I do love myself. This may be the most important gift I have ever given myself. Truly loving myself has allowed me to truly and purely love others.

Meditation became a regular part of my self-care routine. Each day for at least 20 minutes I would sit on my floor on a pillow and meditate. I had been exposed to meditation

during my first round of rehab at Rimrock
Foundation in Billings, Montana. what I
remember most about that first experience is
how I was taught to breathe. It was a guided
meditation and we were told to think about water
pouring out of a pitcher and then being back into
the pitcher. So when you exhale you're expelling
air from the top of your lungs down. As you
inhale you are inhaling air to the very bottom of
your lungs to fill them to the top. This visual
helps me understand proper breathing
techniques for meditation and even exercise. I
also fondly recall how I felt after that first session
of meditation. At 16 or 17 years old having lived
most of my life in some form of twisted agony,
self-doubt and self-sabotaging behavior
meditation brought me a sense of calm. I had
relaxed my mind. I was taking a break and it just
felt amazing. This is why I decided that I needed
to add meditation into my self-care routine as I
continued to choose life.

     These three methodologies helped me
gain a healthier relationship with my emotions,
my mind, and my body. The other intentional
and immediate choice I made was to get
involved with a local church. One of the five
areas of holistic wellness is spiritual. That
doesn't necessarily mean going to church for

everyone but for me, there was a sense of comfort in reaffirming my faith in God. It provided me an opportunity to get involved with my community and even do some good.

After getting to know some of the members of the congregation I was asked to join the Stephen Ministry program a Christian Life Center. The training to become a Stephen Minister is extensive and requires a great amount of introspection. As a Stephen Minister, you are asked to be a sounding board for the pain of someone dealing with the loss of a loved one, a terminal illness or divorce. This is a great responsibility and the training prepared us well to know ourselves and strengthen our relationship with God.

By consistently committing to these new behaviors and letting go of old habits I made significant progress in my healing and growth. Because I was making better choices I started making new friends. Slowly I began surrounding myself with people who not only cared about me but also took an active role in my personal and professional development. I knew in my heart I was good, I loved myself for the first time in my life. I genuinely felt that I, Andrew Carroll, deserved my very best effort. This was an incredibly refreshing feeling that continues to grow and develop within me.

I strive to be honest about all of my failures, not just my criminal history. This can be a difficult task at times because I had done an absolutely amazing job at screwing up prior to choosing life. I've shared these failures so you know you're not alone. I have lived 30 years of setting myself up to fail. The choice I made to live required me to take an intelligent approach to changing my bad habits. It required me to intentionally change my behavior. All of this required immediate action. Do you get as excited as I do when I'm reading a book or watching a movie and the titular line finally arrives? It almost makes me giddy!

Relax, You Got This!

For this exercise I want you to put on some music you find calm and soothing. Not to loud now! You will need to find a comfortable space. This shouldn't be to hard, you are reading a book after all. I like to read in a comfy chair or laying on the couch! When you've gotten comfy and put that music on I want you to gently focus on your breathing. Inhale...Exhale...You will feel the air moving in and out through your nose and mouth. Be mindful of the sensation. After a few breaths I want you to close your eyes, focus on your breathing and just love yourself intensely. You deserve it! Practice this for at least five minutes. If you go longer, AWESOME!

When you are done I want you to write down how you feel in the notebook you have been recording our adventure in!

Chapter 10 - The Three I's

Making an intelligent change is easier for some people. Personally, it took me a lot of screwing up and finding out for myself before I applied any intelligence to my situation. Intelligence is defined as the ability to acquire and apply knowledge and skills. Knowledge and skills are gained through experience. So, for me, to apply my 30 years of screw up experience into a new way of life was intelligent.

I had to take a good long look at what I had been doing to self-sabotage over that time. The choices I made as a child, a teenager and in my 20's that led me into my darkness were all part of my process of becoming Andrew Carroll. The legal system, divorce, bankruptcy, co-parenting, serving in the Air Force, being expelled from high school, being a dad, graduating from college, becoming a leader, winning civilian of the year; each of these things, good and bad, is a part of who I am today. They provided me with the experience necessary to stand as an authority on changing lives.

If you haven't picked it up from reading, I can be rather hard-headed, possibly even stubborn. I always insisted on doing things my own way. When they didn't pan out properly I would generally blame a flaw in the system, unconscionable public policy, or someone having it out for me. When I took an objective step back I realized the common denominator in all of my failures was me. It wasn't policy, the system or anyone else but me making poor choices and continuing self-destructive patterns. As this realization solidified within me I had to examine everything I had put myself through so I could make an intelligent change and break the cycle.

How did I do this? I set intelligent, values-based goals. I looked back at my past behavior and self-sabotage and I identified things that I valued. When you look back on your life you will find defining moments. Moments that your true character shines brightly. Perhaps it was a time you stood up to a bully. Maybe you called out a major safety hazard on a job site even though it had "always been done that way". Could it be a time you volunteered to help a group in the local community?

Even under all your darkness, there is still a light that shines through. I'm a good person who has made poor choices. I still value myself, family, education, hard work, dedication, time and career. I set a goal to graduate from college. I achieved this goal because it aligned with how I value education. I picked myself up and changed my life because I value myself and my family. This aligns with the values of self and family. My kids, my ex-wife and I are all much better off than when we were a toxic family unit.

When I think back on goals I set out of a desire for status or notoriety I never achieved them. This is because I didn't actually care about achieving them. They didn't align with any of my real values. Would it be nice to be a famous movie star? Probably, but I didn't focus my energy into that goal because I didn't really value the end result.

My point is this. Setting intelligent, values-based goals is a surefire way to achieve your own brand of success. Without these intelligent goals, you may succeed here and there, but you will not be maximizing your success and may find yourself disenchanted with your life. So set this book down right now, grab a notepad and a pen and hand write your goals. Plaster them on your mirror, refrigerator and the inside of your door so you see them every time you leave the house.

INTENTIONALLY
DONE ON PURPOSE; DELIBERATE

Intelligently evaluating your past and present so you can maximize your future will only work if you are intentional. This may come as a surprise but I have actually been accused of being intelligent at different points in my life. I am great at picking up new skills or quickly understanding a new task I have just been shown. I was never intentional about applying it to my life. A big part of my personality involves jumping in with both feet regardless of the consequences and figuring out what I needed to do to adapt as the event unfolded. This works for some things but when it comes to life you really need to have a plan in place!

There is a book out there about habits that says something about starting with the end in mind. This is one of the methods we are using here. Setting intelligent, values-based goals allows you to be intentional about achievement.

This is a critical step in breaking your cycle of self-sabotage. Developing a plan you can implement will result in changing your life for the better. As you already have your goals figured out, handwritten, from the last section you can now look at ways to achieve those goals. What are the steps you need to take to get from where you are in your current state to where you want to be in your future state?

Perhaps you set a goal to become more financially stable. This is a great goal! Well, what are the steps involved in becoming more financially stable? First, if you are like most other Americans you would probably need to sit down and create a budget that takes income and all current expenses into consideration. This is a time-consuming process. But you MUST find your current financial state in order to improve it for the future. Once you have your budget figured out (step one) you would then analyze wants, needs, and goals. Perhaps you NEED to make mortgage/rent payments and buy groceries. Perhaps you WANT to buy new clothes. Then you set a goal to save $5,000 in the next six months. You review your budget (step two) and realize that if you stop eating out 8 times per month and only eat out four times per month and don't buy coffee every day you will be saving $600/month. Just those two minor adjustments would boost your savings account by $3,600 in 6 months.

By taking starting with a goal in mind and then working backward you can see how you can take something that may seem "pie in the sky" and break it into completely manageable chunks that pay significant dividends. You are able to be intentional about achieving that goal because you have identified actionable steps that you can take along the path to that goal.

I will be totally honest with you here, my personality and planning have a hard time getting along! I'm a "just go for it" kind of guy. Plans make me a bit nervous but they have significant value. Have you labeled yourself as a "non-planner" as I have? Well, we both need to actively work on that self-talk and bring our values and desires in line with a healthy thought process. We are planners and doers! What an amazing mix of things to be!

Planning out the path to my goals so I could be intentional about changing my life wasn't easy at first. I struggled with it quite a bit. Something that really helped me out was surrounding myself with people that were already where I wanted to be. I asked them the tough questions. I was vulnerable and shared with them my desire to grow and better myself. These people helped me find the path to success in my life. Because of this, I was able to plan out my path of achievement.

My plan involved journaling, spiritual growth, meditation, finances, fitness, nutrition and socializing. This is not a comprehensive list of everything but it is a foundation from which I built myself up. I planned my day around these things. I would journal in the morning and evening. I meditated at least once per day. I worked out five to seven times per week. I prepped my meals and reviewed my budget. I attended church once per week and sometimes attended classes, too. I was intentional about my growth! The great thing about this is that you are being intentional right now! You are reading this book and taking away valuable lessons on changing your life and getting where you want to be!

IMMEDIATELY
AT ONCE; INSTANTLY

The very first I had you identify and write down a list of values based goals. The second I helped you understand the path to intentionally achieving those goals. This wouldn't be called the Three I's if we didn't wrap it up with the final

I! This last I stands for Immediately. Obviously defined as "at once; instantly", this I will have you start sometime next week after you have everything lined out and have your house in order...Absolutely NOT! No way!

The third I in this system has you start RIGHT NOW! For a large part of my life, I slept on my great ideas. Do you remember iPhone docks and docks with alarm clocks? I thought of that idea 3 years before they came to the market. Helmet to helmet communication for motorcycle riders? Also something I thought of before they came to market, or at least before I ever became aware of them. I am sure you have also had a bunch of phenomenal ideas that you didn't capitalize on because while you were waiting, someone else was implementing.

I want to share with you one of the most profound pearls of wisdom I have ever been blessed with. Are you ready? This is a big one:

DONE IS BETTER THAN PERFECT!!!!

Now go back and read that again. And again. And because this is the THREE i's read it one more time for good measure. My point? Get started on creating the change you want in your life RIGHT NOW! TODAY! Don't keep waiting for the "perfect time" because I promise you it isn't going to come. You will never be "ready".

You have a responsibility to yourself to identify your goals, be intentional about achieving them and starting on that today. You are absolutely worth the effort and investment in getting started today. Even in the first I of the system you practiced immediacy. I told you to find a piece of paper and a pen so you could identify your values and create goals. This allowed you to identify the intentional path you would follow to achieve those goals.

It is time for you to let go of fear and accept the abundance that is already yours. You are worth all of it and it starts right now. Journal, meditate and cut off the negative self-talk. Make a plan for the gym and nutrition and solidify healthy tangible habits. Don't wait. Go! Get started! Begin the process of building your very best you, now!

You've Already Started

Throughout this book I've asked you to write down thoughts, feelings and experiences in a notebook. I know you've been following along on these exercises so I have a surprise for you. Are you ready? You have already created a journal full of intimate wisdom about who you are and where you want to go in life! It is my hope that you will continue to write in your journal and show yourself all the love, compassion and accountability you deserve.

Another bit of wisdom for you; You deserve ALL the love, compassion and accountability! If you find yourself doubting things, that is okay. This is a completely normal part of the healing process. When you do feel doubt it is imperative that you put into action the tools and healthy mechanisms you have identified through the exercises in your journal. My friend, welcome to the love and self-improvement movement!

Epilogue - I Love You

I believe in you so much it brings tears to my eyes. We, as humans, are absolutely incredible beings that are capable of so much compassion, love, and goodness. We have been bombarded for most of our lives with inputs that make us feel small and ashamed. If you are anything like me you have or are currently struggling with negativity and self-worth. I know your pain. You are not alone.

I existed in a space where I felt small and unworthy for 31 years of my life. I shared with you my kindergarten experience. The first time I was made to feel small. I shared with you my youth and adult mistakes. All of these things were incredibly painful experiences in my life. I never thought for a moment as I was dwelling in this dark, muddy cave of isolation, that the experiences that challenged me, broke me and forced me to struggle would bring me to where I am today.

It is my greatest hope that what I have shared with you here resonates within your soul. I want you to feel my loving energy within the pages of this book. I want you to know that you are not alone in any trial or difficulty you face. There are a ton of people in your life that support your positive and healthy growth. I am one of them. But I am not enough! This transformation is based solely on the work you are willing to do.

An interesting point of clarity I want to share with you is this; as you grow and become healthier there will be people in your life that try to drag you back down. The old adage of crabs in a bucket comes to mind here. Crabs in a bucket will not let an individual crab climb out of the bucket. As soon as one crab tries to better its situation by taking the action of climbing out the other crabs will grab it and drag it back into the bucket. For you and I darkness and self-sabotage can become our bucket and the people in our lives can definitely be the other crabs.

Surround yourself with people who are not crabs and don't like buckets and you will find yourself being loved, invested in and mentored by incredible humans who are already living the life you want for yourself.

Fellow traveler, I love and cherish you. The light and love within me recognizes, respects and honors the light and love within you. Namaste.

ABOUT THE AUTHOR

The first time I was ever made to feel small was my first day of Kindergarten. I carried this with me for the next 26 years of my life. In October 2017 I made the choice to live. My name is Andrew Carroll and I am a father, son, leader, coach, speaker, influencer and human. Like you I have struggled with self-sabotage and fear most of my life. I'm here to tell you that with Intelligent, Intentional and Immediate action you can break the negative cycles and live your best life. There is no magic bullet. It takes work. Consistent, honest work.

Right now I live in Utah. I love to travel. Adventure and barefeet speak to my soul. I'd love to meet you. New people are an incredible opportunity to learn. My hope for humanity is that we all learn to show respect for the person and approach adversity with an open mind. Life isn't all sunshine and rainbows and I completely understand that. Read the book and you'll see why. However, I believe that the journey we are on is all about learning the lessons placed in front of us. When we ignore those...well, disaster ensues.

I hope you enjoy the book. How cool would it be if you are in a bookstore checking out this About the Author section right now?!

Namaste <3

Made in the USA
Middletown, DE
30 May 2020